ROBERT GREENE
GROATS-VVORTH OF
WITTE
THE REPENTANCE OF
ROBERT GREENE
1592

ELIZABETHAN AND JACOBEAN QUARTOS

ELIZABETHAN AND JACOBEAN QUARTOS
EDITED BY G. B. HARRISON

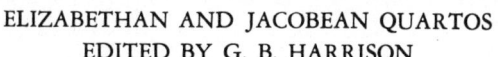

ROBERT GREENE, M.A.

GROATS-VVORTH OF WITTE,
bought with a million of Repentance

THE REPENTANCE OF
ROBERT GREENE

1592

BARNES & NOBLE, Inc.
New York, New York

PR
2544
.G7
1592b

This edition published in 1966
by Barnes & Noble, Inc.
is reproduced from the series
BODLEY HEAD QUARTOS
published by
John Lane The Bodley Head Ltd., London
between 1922 and 1926

Note

THE ORIGINAL of this text is in the British Museum (C. 57. b. 42). The few misprints which have been corrected in the text are noted on page 52.

G. B. H.

Printed in the United States of America

GREENES,
GROATS-WORTH
of witte, bought with a million of Repentance.

Describing the follie of youth, the falshood of make-shifte flatterers, the miserie of the negligent, and mischiefes of deceiuing Courtezans.

Written before his death and published at his dyeing request.

Fœlicem fuiße infaustum.

LONDON
Imprinted for William Wright.
1 5 9 2.

The Printer to the Gentle Readers.

I HAUE published here Gentlemen for your mirth and benefite *Greenes* groates worth of wit. VVith sundry of his pleasant discourses, ye haue beene before delighted: But nowe hath death giuen a period to his pen: onely this happened into my handes which I haue published for your pleasures: Accept it fauourably because it was his last birth and not least worth: In my poore opinion. But I will cease to praise that which is aboue my conceipt, & leaue it selfe to speak for it selfe: and so abide your learned censuring.

Yours VV. VV. /[A3

To the Gentlemen Readers.

GENTLEMEN. The Swan sings melodiously before death, that in all his life time vseth but a iarring sound. Greene though able inough to write, yet deeplyer serched with sicknes than euer heeretofore, sendes you his Swanne like songe, for that he feares he shall neuer againe carroll to you woonted loue layes, neuer againe discouer to you youths pleasures. How euer yet sicknesse, riot, Incontinence, haue at once shown their extremitie yet if I recouer, you shall all see, more fresh sprigs, then euer sprang from me, directing you how to liue, yet not diswading ye from loue. This is the last I haue writ, and I feare me the last I shall writ. And how euer I haue beene censured for some of my former bookes, yet Gentlemen I protest, they were as I had speciall information. But passing them, I commend this to your fauourable censures, that like an Embrion | [A3ᵛ] *without shape, I feare me will be thrust into the world. If I liue to end it, it shall be otherwise : if not, yet will I commend it to your courtesies, that you may as well be acquainted with my repentant death, as you haue lamented my careles course of life. But as* Nemo ante obitum felix, *so* Acta Exitus probat: *Beseeching therefore so to be deemed heereof as I deserue, I leaue the worke to your likinges, and leaue you to your delightes.*

GREENES
GROATES-VVORTH
OF WIT.

IN an Iland bounded with the Ocean there was somtime a Cittie situated, made riche by Marchandize, and populous by long peace, the name is not mentioned in the Antiquarie, or els worne out by times Antiquitie, what it was it greatly skilles not, but therein thus it happened. An old new made Gentleman herein dwelt, of no small credit, exceeding wealth, and large conscience: hee had gathered from many to bestow vpon one, for though he had two sonnes he esteemed but one, that being as himselfe, brought vp to be golds bondman, was therefore held heire apparant of his il gathered goods.

The other was a Scholler, and maried to a proper Gentlewoman and therfore least regarded, for tis an old sayd saw: To learning & law, thers no greater foe than they that nothing know: yet / [B1 was not the father altogether vnlettered, for he had good experience in a *Nouerint*, and by the vniuersall tearmes therein contained, had driuen many a yoong Gentleman to seeke vnknowen countries, wise he was, for he boare office in his parish and sat as formally in his foxfurd gowne, as if he had been a very vpright dealing Burges: he was religious too, neuer without a booke at his belt, and a bolt in his mouthe, readye to shoote through his sinfull neighbor.

And Latin hee had some where learned, which though it were but little, yet was it profitable, for he had this Philosophye written in a ring, *Tu tibi cura*, which precept he curiously obserued, being in selfeloue so religious, as he held it no poynt of charitie to part with any thing, of whiche hee liuing might make vse.

But as all mortall thinges are momentarie, and no certaintie can bee found in this vncertaine world: so *Gorinius*, (for that shall bee this vsurers name) after manye a gowtie pang that had pincht his exterior partes, many a curse of the people that moũted into heauens presence, was at last with his last summons, by a deadly disease arrested, wher-against when hee had long contended, and was by Phisitions giuen ouer, he cald his two sonnes before him: and willing to performe the olde prouerb *Qualis vita finis Ita*, he thus prepard him-selfe, and admonished them. My sonnes (for so your mother sayde ye were) and so I assure my selfe one of you is, and of the other I will make no doubt. [B1ᵛ

You se the time is com, which I thought would/ neuer haue aproched and we must now be sepe-rated, I feare neuer to meete againe. This sixteene yeares dayly haue I liude vexed with disease: and might I liue sixteene more, howe euer miserably, I should thinke it happye. But death is relentlesse, and will not be intreated witles: and knowes not what good my gold might doo him: senseles, & hath no pleasure in the delightfull places I would offer him. In briefe, I thinke he hath with this foole my eldest sonne been brought vp in the vniuersitie, and therefore accounts that in riches is no vertue. But thou my son, (laying then his hand on the yongers head) haue thou another spirit: for without wealth, life is a death: what is gentry if welth be wanting, but bace seruile beggerie. Some comfort yet it is vnto me, to thinke how many Gallants sprunge of noble parents, haue croucht to *Gorinius* to haue sight of his gold: O gold, desired gold, admired gold: and haue lost their patrimonies to *Gorinius*, because they haue not returned by their day that adored creature: How manye Schollers haue written rymes in *Gorinius* praise, and receiued (after long capping and reuerence) a sixpeny reward in signe of my superficial liberality. Breefly my yong *Lucanio* how I haue beene reurenst thou seest, when honester men I confesse haue been sett farre off: for to bee rich is to bee any thing, wise, honest, worshipful, or what not. I tel thee my sonne: when I came first to this Citie my whole wardrop was onely a sute of white sheepe skins, my wealth an old groat,

my woonning, the wide world. At this instant (O
greefe to part with it) I haue in ready / coine [B2
three-score thousand pound, in plate and Iewels
xv. thousand; in Bondes and specialties as much, in
land nine hundred pound by the yeere: all which,
Lucanio I bequeath to thee, only I reserue for
Roberto thy wel red brother an old groat, (being y^e
stocke I first began with) wherewith I wish him to
buy a groats-worth of wit: for he in my life hath
reprooud my manner of life, and therefore at my
death, shall not be contaminated with corrupt
gaine. Here by the way Gentlemen must I
digresse to shewe the reason of *Gorinius* present
speach: *Roberto* being come from the Academie,
to visit his father, there was a great feast prouided:
where for table talke, *Roberto* knowing his father
and most of the company to be execrable vsurers,
inuayed mightely against that abhorred vice, inso-
muche that hee vrged teares from diuers of their
eyes, and compunction in some of their harts.
Dinner being past, he comes to his father, request-
ing him to take no offence at his liberall speach,
seeing what he had vttred was truth. Angry sonne
(said he) no by my honestie (and that is som what
I may say to you) but vse it still, and if thou canst
perswade any of my neighbours from lending vppon
vsurie I shuld haue the more customers: to which
when *Roberto* would haue replyde hee shut himselfe into his study, and fell to tell ouer his mony.

This was *Robertos* offence: now returne, wee to sicke *Gorinius*, who after he had thus vnequally distributed his goods and possessions, began to aske his sonnes how they liked his bequestes, either seemed agreed, and *Roberto* vrged him with / nothing more than repentance of his sinn- [B2ᵛ loke: to thine owne said he, fonde boy, & come my *Lucanio*, let me giue thee good counsell before my death: as for you sir, your bookes are your counsellors, and therefore to them I bequeathe you. Ah *Lucanio*, my onely comfort, because I hope thou wilt as thy father be a gatherer, let me blesse thee before I dye. Multiply in welth my sonne by any meanes thou maist, onely flye Alchymie, for therein are more deceites than her beggerlye Artistes haue words, and yet are the wretches more talkatiue than women. But my meaning is, thou shouldest not stand on conscience in causes of profit, but heap treasure vpon treasure, for the time of neede: yet seem to be deuout, els shalt thou be held vyle, frequent holy exercises graue companie, and aboue al vse the conuersation of yoong Gentlemen, who are so wedded to prodigalitie, that once in a quarter necissitie knocks at their chamber doores: profer them kindnesse to relieue their wants, but be sure of good assurance: giue faire wordes till dayes of paiment come, & then vse my course, spare none: what though they tell of conscience (as a number will talke) looke but

into the dealinges of the world, and thou shalt see
it is but idle words. Seest thou not many perish in
the streetes, and fall to theft for neede: whom small
succor woulde releeue, then where is conscience,
and why art thou bound to vse it more than other
men? Seest thou not daylie forgeries periuries,
oppressions, rackinges of the poore, raisinges of
rents, inhauncing of duties euen by them that
should be al conscience, if they ment as they
speake: / but *Lucanio* if thou read well this [B3
booke (and with that hee reacht him *Machiauels*
workes at large) thou shalt se, what tis to be so
foole-holy as to make scruple of conscience where
profit presents it selfe.

Besides, thou hast an instance by the threedbare
brother here, who willing to do no wrong, hath
lost his childes right: for who woulde wish any
thinge to him, that knowes not how to vse it.

So much *Lucanio* for conscience: & yet I know
not whats the reason, but some-what stinges mee
inwardly when I speake of it. I father said *Roberto*, it is the worme of conscience, that vrges you
at the last houre to remember your life, that
eternall life may followe your repentance. Out
foole (sayd this miserable father), I feele it now, it
was onelye a stitch. I will forwarde with my exhortation to *Lucanio*. As I said my sonne, make spoyle
of yoong Gallants, by insinuating thy selfe amongst
them, & be not mooued to thinke their Auncestors

were famous, but consider thine were obscure, and that thy father was the first Gentleman of the Name: *Lucanio*, thou art yet a Bacheler, and soe keepe thee till thou meete with one that is thy equal, I meane in wealth: regarde not beautie, it is but a bayte to entice thine neighbors eye: and the most faire are commonlye most fond, vse not too many familiars, for few prooue frendes, and as easie it is to weigh the wind, as to diue into the thoughtes of worldlye glosers. I tell thee *Lucanio*, I haue seene four-scoore winters besides the od seuen, yet saw I neuer him, that I esteemed as my friend but gold, that desired creature, whom I haue so deerly loued, / and found so firme a [B3ᵛ] frind, as nothing to me hauing it hath beene wanting. No man but may thinke deerly of a true frend, & so do I of it laying it vnder sure locks, and lodging my heart there-with.

But now (Ah my *Lucanio*) now must I leaue it, and to thee I leaue it with this lessen, loue none but thy selfe, if thou wilt liue esteemd. So turning him to his studdy, where his cheife treasure lay, he loud cryde out in the wise mans woords, *O mors quam amara*, O death how bitter is thy memory to him that hath al pleasures in this life, & so with two or three lamentable grones hee left his life: and to make short worke, was by *Lucanio* his sonne interd, as the custome is with some solemnitie: But leauing him that hath left the world to him that censureth of euery worldly man, passe wee to his sonnes: and se how his long laid vp store is by *Lucanio* lookyd into. The youth was of condition simple, shamfast, & flexible to any counsaile, which *Roberto* perceiuing, and pondering howe little was lefte to him, grew into an inward contempt of his fathers vnequall legacie, and determinate resolution to work *Lucanio* al possible iniurie, herevpon thus conuerting the sweetnes of his studdye to the sharpe thirst of reuenge, he (as Enuie is seldome idle) sought out fit companions to effect his vnbrotherly resolution. Neither in such a case is ill company far to seek, for ye Sea hath scarce so ieoperdies, as populous Citties haue deceiuing Syrens, whose eies are Adamants, whose words are witchcraftes, whose doores lead downe to death. With one of these female serpents *Roberto* consorts, and / they conclude what euer [B4 they compassed equally to sharre to their contentes. This match made, *Lucanio* was by his brother brought to the bush, where he had scarce pruned his winges, but hee was fast limd, and *Roberto* had what he expected. But that wee may keepe forme, you shall heare howe it fortuned.

Lucanio being on a time verie pensiue, his brother brake with him in these termes. I wonder *Lucanio* why you are disconsolate, that want not any thinge in the worlde that may worke your content. If wealth may delight a man, you are with that sufficiently furnisht: if credit may procure any comfort, your word I knowe well, is as well accepted as any mans obligation: in this Citie, are faire buildings and pleasant gardens, and cause of solace, of them I am assured you haue your choyce. Consider brother you are yoong, then plod not altogether in meditating on our fathers precepts: which howseuer they sauored of profit, were most vnsauerly to one of your yeares applied. You must not thinke but sundrye marchants of this Citie expect your company, sundry Gentlemen desire your familiaritie, & by cõuersing with such, you wil be accounted a Gentleman: otherwise a pesant, if ye liue thus obscurely. Besides, which I had almost forgot and then had al the rest beene nothing, you are a man by nature furnished with all exquisite proportion, worthy the loue of any courtly lady, be she neuer so amorous: you haue wealth to maintaine her, of women not little longed for: wordes to court her you shall not want, for my selfe will be / your secretarie. Breefely [B4^v why stand I to distinguish abilitie in perticularities, when in one word it may be said which no man can gainsay, *Lucanio* lacketh nothing to delight a wife, nor any thing but a wife to delight him? My yoong maister being thus clawd, and pufft vp with his owne praise, made no longer delay, but hauing on his holidaie hose hee trickt himselfe vp and like a fellowe that meant good sooth, he clapt hys brother on the shoulder and said. Faith brother *Roberto*, and ye say the worde lets goe seeke a wife while tis hoat, both of vs together, Ile pay well, and I dare tourne you loose to say as well as any of them all, well Ile doo my best said *Roberto* and since ye are so forwarde lets goe nowe and try your good fortune.

With this foorth they walke, and *Roberto* went directly toward the house where *Lamilia* (for so wee call the Curtizan) kept her hospitall, which was in the suburbes of the Citie, pleasantly seated, and made more delectable by a pleasaunt garden wherin it was scituate. No soner come they within ken, but Mistris *Lamilia* like a cunning angler made readye her change of baytes that shee might effect *Lucanios* bane: and to begin she discouered from her window her beauteous enticing face, and taking a lute in her hand that shee might the rather allure, shee soung this sonnet with a delicious voyce,/ [C1

Lamilias song.

Fie fie on blind fancie,
It hinders youths ioy :
Faire virgins learne by me,
To count loue a toy.
When loue learnd first the A B C of delight,
And knew no figures, nor conceited phrase :
He simply gaue to due desert her right,
He lead not louers in darke winding wayes,

He plainely wild to loue, or flatly answerd no,
But now who lists to proue shall find it nothing so,
  Fie fie then on fancie,
  It hinders youths ioy,
  Faire virgins learne by me,
  To count loue a toy.
For since he learnd to vse the Poets pen,
He learnd likewise with smoothing words to faine,
Witching chast eares with trothles tungs of men,
And wronged faith with falshood and disdaine.
  He giues a promise now, anon he sweareth no,
  Who listeth for to proue shall find his changings so,
    Fie fie then on fancie,
    It hinders youthes ioy,
    Faire virgins learne by me,
    To count loue a toy./ [C1ᵛ]

While this painted sepulcher was shadowing her corrupting guilt, Hiena-like alluring to destruction, *Roberto* and *Lucanio* vnder her windowe kept euen pace with euery stop of her instrument, but especially my yoong Ruffler, (that before time like a birde in a cage had beene prentise for three liues or one and twentie yeares at lest to extreame Avarice his deceased father) O twas a world to see howe hee sometyme simperd it, striuing to sett a countenance on his new turnd face, that it might seeme of wainscot proofe, to behold her face without blushing: anone he would stroke his bow-bent-leg,

as if he ment to shoote loue arrows from his
shins: then wypt his chin (for his beard was not
yet growen) with a gold wrought handkercher,
whence of purpose he let fall a handfull of Angels.
This golden shower was no sooner raind, but
Lamilia ceast her song, and *Roberto* (assureing
himselfe the foole was caught) came to *Lucanio*
(that stood now as one that had stard *Medusa* in
the face) and awaked him from his amazement
with these wordes. What in a traunce brother?
whence springs these dumps? are ye amazd at this
obiect? or long ye to become loues subiect? Is
there not difference betweene this delectable life,
and the imprisonment you haue all your life
hethertoo indured? If the sight and hearing of
this harmonyous beautie worke in you effects of
wonder, what will the possession of so deuine an
essence, wherein beautie & Art dwell in their
perfectest excellence. Brother said *Lucanio* lets
vse fewe wordes, and shee be no more then a
woman, I trust youle helpe / me to win her? [C2
and if you doe, well, I say no more but I am yours
till death vs depart, and what is mine shall be
yours world without end Amen.

Roberto smiling at his simplenes, helpte him to
gather vppe his dropt gold, and without anye more
circumstance, led him to *Lamilias* house: for of
such places it may be said as of hell.

Noctes atque dies patet atri ianua ditis.

So their dores are euer open to entice youth to distruction. They were no sooner entred but *Lamilia* her selfe like a seconde *Helen*, court like begins to salute *Roberto*, yet did her wandring eie glance often at *Lucanio*: the effect of her intertainment consisted in these tearmes, that to her simple house Signor *Roberto* was welcome, & his brother the better welcom for his sake: albeit his good report confirmde by his present demeaner were of it selfe enough to giue him deserued entertainement in any place how honorable soeuer: mutuall thankes returnd, they lead this prodigall child into a parlor garnished with goodly portratures of amiable personages: nere which an excellent consort of musike began at their entraunce to play. *Lamilia* seeing *Lucanio* shamefast, tooke him by the hand, and tenderly wringing him vsed these wordes. Beleeue me Gentleman, I am very sorie that our rude entertainment is such, as no way may worke your content, for this I haue noted since your first entering that your countenance hath beene heauie, and the face being the glasse of the hart, assures me the same is not quiet: would ye wish any thing heere that might content you, say / but the word, and assure ye of present [C2ʳ diligence to effect your full delight. *Lucanio* being so farre in loue, as he perswaded himselfe without her grant he could not liue, had a good meaninge to vtter his minde but wanting fit wordes, he stood

like a trewant that lackt a prompter, or a plaier
that being out of his part at his first entrance, is
faine to haue the booke to speak what he should
performe. Which *Roberto* perceiuing, replied thus
in his behalfe: Madame the Sunnes brightnesse
daisleth the beholders eies, the maiestie of Gods,
amazeth humane men, *Tullie* Prince of Orators
once fainted though his cause were good, and hee
that tamed monsters stoode amated at Beauties
ornaments: Then blame not this yoong man
though he replied not, for he is blinded with the
beautie of your sunne darkening eies, made mute
with the celestiall organe of your voyce, and feare
of that rich ambush of amber colored dartes, whose
poyntes are leueld against his hart. Well Signor
Roberto said shee, how euer you interpret their
sharpe leuell, be sure they are not bent to doo him
hurt, and but that modestie blindes vs poore
maydens from vttering the inward sorrow of our
mindes, perchance the cause of greefe is ours how
euer men do colour, for as I am a virgin I protest,
(and therewithall shee tainted her cheekes with a
vermilion blush) I neuer saw Gentleman in my life
in my eie so gratious as is *Lucanio* only this is my
greefe, that either I am dispised for that he scornes
to speak, or els (which is my greater sorrow) I
feare he cannot speake. Not speake Gentlewoman
quoth *Lu/canio* that were a iest indeed, yes I [C3
thanke God I am sound of wind and lym, only my

hart is not as it was wont: but and you be as good as your word that will soone be well, and so crauing ye of more acquaintance, in token of my plaine meaning receiue this diamond, which my old father loud deerely: and with that deliuered her a ringe wherein was a poynted diamonde of wonderfull worth. Which she accepting with a lowe conge, returnd him a silke Riband for a fauour tyde with a true loues knot, which he fastened vnder a faire Iewel on his Beuer felt.

After this *Diomedis & Glauci permutatio*, my yong master waxed crancke, and the musike continuing, was very forward in dauncing, to shew his cunning: and so desiring them to play on a hornepipe, laid on the pauement lustely with his leaden heeles, coruetting, like a steede of *Signor Roccoes* teaching, & wanted nothing but bels, to be a hobbyhorse in a morrice. Yet was he soothed in his folly, and what euer he did *Lamilia* counted excellent: her prayse made him proude, in so much that if hee had not beene intreated, hee would rather haue died in his daunce, then left off to shew his mistris delight. At last reasonably perswaded, seeing the table furnished, hee was content to cease, and settle him to his victuals, on which (hauing before labored) hee fed lustely, especially of a Woodcocke pye, wherewith *Lamilia* his caruer, plentifully plied him. Full dishes hauing furnisht empty stomackes, and *Lucanio* therby got leisure to talke, falles to discourse of his wealth, his landes, his bondes, his ability, / and how himselfe with [C3ᵛ all he had, was at madame *Lamilias* disposing: desiring her afore his brother to tell him simply what she meant. *Lamilia* replied My sweet *Lucanio*, how I esteeme of thee mine eies do witnes, that like handmaides, haue attended thy beauteous face, euer since I firste behelde thee: yet seeing loue that lasteth, gathereth by degrees his liking: let this for that suffice, if I finde thee firme, *Lamilia* wilbe faithfull: if fleeting, shee must of necessity be infortunate: that hauing neuer seene any whome before she could affect, she should be of him iniuriously forsaken. Nay said *Lucanio*, I dare say my brother here will giue his woord for that I accept your own said *Lamilia*: for with me your credite is better than your brothers. *Roberto* brake off their amorous prattle with this speech. Sith either of you are of other so fond at the first sight, I doubt not but time will make your loue more firme. Yet madame *Lamilia* although my brother and you bee thus forward, some crosse chaunce may come: for *Multa cadunt inter calicem supremaq; labe.* And for a warning to teach you both wit, Ile tell you an old wiues tale.

Before ye goe on with our tale (qd Mistris *Lamilia*) let me giue ye a caueat by the wey, which shall be figured in a fable.

Lamilias Fable.

THE Foxe on a time came to visite the Gray,
partly for kindered cheefly for craft: and
finding the hole emptie of all other company,
sauing only one Badger enquired the cause of his
solitarinesse: hee dis/cribed, the sodaine death of [C4
his dam and sire with the rest of his consortes. The
Fox made a Friday face, counterfeiting sorrow:
but concludinge that deaths stroke was vneuitable
perswaded him to seeke som fit mate wherwith to
match. The badger soone agreed, so forth they
went, and in their way met with a wãton ewe
stragling from the fold: the foxe bad the Badger
play the tall stripling, & strout on his tiptoes: for
(qd he) this ewe is lady of al these lawnds and her
brother cheefe belweather of sundry flockes. To
bee short by the Foxes perswasion there would bee
a perpetuall league, betweene her harmeles kindred, and all other deuouring beastes, for that the
Badger was to them all allied: seduced she yeelded,
and the Fox conducted them to the Badgers habitation. Wher drawing her aside vnder color of
exhortation, puld out her throat to satisfie his
greedy thirst. Here I shoulde note, a yoonge
whelpe that viewed their walke, infourmed the
shepheardes of what hapned. They followed, and
trained the Foxe and Badger to the hole, the Foxe
afore had craftely conuaid himselfe away, the

shepheards found the Badger rauing for the ewes murther, his lamẽtation being held for counterfet, was by the shepherds dogs werried. The Foxe escaped: the Ewe was spoiled, and euer since betweene the Badgers and dogs hath continued a mortall enmitie: And now be aduized, *Roberto* (qd she) go forward with your tale, seek not by sly insinuation to turne our mirth to sorrow. Go to *Lamilia* (qd he) you feare what I meane not, but howe euer yee take it, Ile forward with my tale./

[C4ᵛ]

Robertoes Tale.

IN the North partes there dwelt an olde Squier, that had a young daughter his heire; who had (as I knowe Madam *Lamilia* you haue had) many youthfull Gentlemen that long time sued to obtaine her loue. But she knowing her own perfections (as women are by nature proud) would not to any of them vouchsafe fauour: insomuch that they perceiuing her relentlesse, shewed themselues not altogether witlesse, but left her to her fortune, when they found her frowardnes. At last it fortuned among other strangers, a Farmers sonne visited her Fathers house: on whom at the first sight she was enamoured, he likewise on her. Tokens of loue past betweene them, either acquainted others parentes of their choise, and they kindly gaue their consent. Short tale to make, married they were, and great solempnitie was at the wedding feast. A yong Gentleman, that had beene long a suiter to her, vexing that the Sonne of a Farmer should bee so preferd, cast in his minde by what meanes (to marre their merriment) hee might steale away the Bride. Hereupon he confers with an olde Beldam, called Mother *Gunby*, dwelling thereby, whose counsell hauing taken, he fell to his practise, and proceeded thus. In the after noone, when dauncers were verie busie, he takes the Bride by the hande, and after a turne or two, tels her in her eare, he had a secret to impart vnto her, appointing her in any wise in the euening to find a time to confer with him: she promist she would, and so they parted. Then goes hee to the Bridegroome, & with / protestations [D1 of entire affect, protests that the great sorrowe hee takes at that which hee must vtter, wheron depended his especiall credit, if it were known the matter by him should be discouered. After the Bridegrooms promise of secrecie, the gentleman tels him, that a frend of his receiued that morning from the Bride a Letter, wherein shee willed him with some sixteene horse to await her comming at a Parke side, for that she detested him in her heart as a base countrey hynde, with whome her Father compeld her to marry. The Bridegroome almost out of his wits, began to bite his lip. Nay, sayth the Gentleman, if you will by me bee aduizde, you shall salue her credit, win her by kindnes, and yet preuent her wanton complot. As how said the Bridegroome? Mary thus saide the Gentleman: In the euening (for till the guests be gone, she intends not to gad) get you on horsebacke, and seeme to bee of the companie that attendes her comming, I am appoynted to bring her from the house to the Parke, and from thence fetch a winding compasse of a mile about, but to turne vnto olde Mother *Gunbyes* house, where her Louer my friend abydes: when she alights, I will conduct her to a chamber farre from his lodging; but when the lights are out, and shee expects her adulterous copesmate, your selfe (as reason is) shall proue her bedfellow, where priuately you may reprooue her, and in the morning earely returne home without trouble. As for the Gentleman my friend, I will excuse her absence to him, by saying, she mockt me with her Mayde in steade of her selfe, whome when I knew at her alighting, I disdained to bring her vnto his presence. The Bridegroome gaue his hand eit shoulde be so./ [D1ᵛ

Now by the way you must vnderstand, this Mother *Gunby* had a daughter, who all that day sate heauily at home with a willow garland, for that the Bridegroome (if hee had dealt faithfully) should haue wedded her before any other. But men (*Lamilia*) are vnconstant, money now a dayes makes the match, or else the match is marde.

But to the matter: the Bridegroome and the
Gentleman thus agreed: he tooke his time, con-
ferd with the Bride, perswaded her that her
husband (notwithstanding his faire shew at the
marriage) had sworne to his olde sweet heart, their
neighbour *Gunbyes* daughter, to bee that night her
bedfellow: and if she would bring her Father, his
Father, and other friendes to the house at mid-
night, they should find it so.

At this the young Gentlewoman inwardly vext
to bee by a peasant so abusde, promist if she saw
likelyhood of his slipping away, that then she
would doo according as he directed.

All this thus sorting, the old womans daughter
was trickly attyrde ready to furnish this pageant,
for her old mother prouided all things necessary.

Well, Supper past, daunsing ended, and the
guests would home, and the Bridegroome pretend-
ing to bring some friend of his home, got his horse,
and to the Parke side he rode, and staide with the
horsemen that attended the Gentleman.

Anon came *Marian* like mistris Bride, and
mounted behind the Gentleman, away they post,
fetch their compasse, & at last alight at the olde
wiues house, where sodenly she is conuayd to her
chamber, & the bridegroome sent to keep her
company, wher he had scarse deuisd how / to [D2
begin his exhortation: but the Father of his Bryde
knockt at the chamber doore. At which being

somewhat amazed, yet thinking to turne it to a ieast, sith his Wife (as hee thought) was in bed with him, hee opened the doore, saying: Father, you are hartily welcome, I wonder how you found vs out heere; this deuise to remooue our selues, was with my wiues consent, that wee might rest quietly without the Maides and Batchelers disturbing. But wheres your Wife said the Gentleman? why heere in bed saide hee. I thought (quoth the other) my daughter had beene your wife, for sure I am to day shee was giuen you in marriage. You are merrely disposed, said the Bridegroome, what thinke you I haue another wife? I thinke but as you speake quoth the Gentleman, for my daughter is below, and you say your wife is in the bed. Below (said he) you are a merry man, and with that casting on a night gowne, hee went downe, where when he saw his wife, the Gentleman his Father, and a number of his friends assembled, hee was so confounded, that how to behaue himselfe he knew not; onely he cryde out that he was deceiued. At this the old woman arises, and making her selfe ignoraunt of all the whole matter, inquires the cause of that sodayne tumult. When she was told the new Bridegroome was founde in bed with her daughter, she exclaimd against so great an iniurie. *Marian* was calde in quorum: shee iustified, it was by his allurement: he being condemnd by all their consents, was adiudged vnworthy to haue the Gentlewoman vnto his Wife, and compeld (for escaping of punishment) to marrie *Marian*: and the young Gentleman (for his care in discouering the Farmers sonnes lewdnes) was recompenst with the Gentlewomans euer during loue./ [D2ᵛ

Quoth *Lamilia*, and what of this? Nay nothing said *Roberto*, but that I haue told you the effects of sodaine loue: yet the best is, my brother is a maidenly Batchler; and for your selfe, you haue not beene troubled with many suiters. The fewer the better, said *Lucanio*. But brother, I con you little thanke for this tale, heereafter I pray you vse other table talke. Lets then end talk, quoth *Lamilia*, and you (signior *Lucanio*) and I will go to the Chesse. To Chesse, said he, what meane you by that? It is a game, said she, that the first daunger is but a checke, the worst, the giuing of a mate. Well, said *Roberto*, that game yee haue beene at already then, for you checkt him first with your beauty, & gaue your selfe for mate to him by your bounty. Thats wel taken brother, said *Lucanio*, so haue we past our game at Chesse. Wil ye play at Tables then, said she? I cannot, quoth hee, for I can goe no further with my game, if I be once taken. Will ye play then at cards. I said he, so it bee at one and thirtie. That fooles game, said she? Wele all to hazard, said *Roberto*, and brother you shall make one for an houre or two: content quoth he. So to dice they went, and fortune so fauored *Lucanio*, that while they continued square play, hee was no looser. Anone coosenage came about, and his Angels being double winged, flew clean from before him. *Lamilia* being the winner, preparde a banquet; which finished, *Roberto* aduisde his brother to departe home, and to furnish himselfe with more Crownes, least hee were outcrackt with new commers.

Lucanio loath to be outcountenanst, followed his aduise, desiring to attend his returne, which hee before had determined vnrequested: For as soone as his brothers backe was turned, *Roberto* begins to recken with *La / milia*, to bee a sharer [D3 as well in the money deceitfully wonne, as in the Diamond so wilfully giuen. But she, *secundum mores meretricis*, iested thus with the scholler. Why *Roberto*, are you so well read, and yet shewe your selfe so shallow witted, to deeme women so weake of conceit, that they see not into mens demerites. Suppose (to make you my stale to catch the woodcocke your brother) that my tongue ouer-running myne intent, I spake of liberall rewarde: but what I promist, theres the point; at least what I part with I will be well aduisde. It may be you will thus reason: Had not *Roberto* traind *Lucanio* vnto *Lamilias* lure, *Lucanio* had not now beene *Lamilias* pray: therefore sith by *Roberto* she possesseth the prize, *Roberto* merites an equal part. Monstrous absurd if so you reason; as wel you may reason thus: *Lamilias* dog hath kild her a Deere, therefore his Mistris must make him a pastie. No poore pennilesse Poet, thou art beguilde in mee, and yet I wonder how thou couldst, thou hast beene so often beguilde. But it fareth with licentious men, as with the chased Bore in the stream, who being greatly refresht with swimming, neuer feeleth anie smart vntill hee perish recurelesly wounded with his owne weapons. Reasonlesse *Roberto*, that hauing but a brokers place, askest a lenders reward. Faithles *Roberto*, that hast attempted to betray thy brother, irreligiously forsaken thy Wife, deseruedly been in thy fathers eie an abiect: thinkst thou *Lamilia* so loose, to consort with one so lewd. No hypocrite, the sweet Gentleman thy brother, I will till death loue, & thee while I liue, loath. This share *Lamilia* giues thee, other getst thou none.

As *Roberto* would haue replide, *Lucanio* approcht: / to whom *Lamilia* discourst the whole [D3ᵛ deceipt of his brother, & neuer rested intimating malitious arguments, til *Lucanio* vtterly refusde *Roberto* for his brother, & for euer forbad him his house. And when he would haue yeelded reasons, and formed excuse, *Lucanios* impatience (vrgd by her importunate malice) forbad all reasoning with them that was reasonlesse, and so giuing him Iacke Drums intertainment, shut him out of doores: whom we will follow, & leaue *Lucanio* to the mercie of *Lamilia*. *Roberto* in an extreme extasie, rent his haire, curst his destenie, blamd his trechery, but most of all exclaimd against *Lamilia*: and in her against all enticing Curtizans, in these tearms.

What meant the Poets in inuectiue verse,
To sing Medeas shame, and Scillas pride,
Calipsoes charmes, by which so many dyde?
Onely for this their vices they rehearse,
That curious wits which in this world conuerse,
May shun the dangers and enticing shoes,
Of such false Syrens, those home-breeding foes,
That from the eyes their venim do disperse.
So soone kils not the Basiliske with sight,
The Vipers tooth is not so venemous,
The Adders tung not halfe so dangerous,
As they that beare the shadow of delight,
Who chaine blind youths in tramels of their haire,
Till wast bring woe, and sorrow hast despaire.

With this he laid his head on his hand, and leant his elbow on the earth, sighing out sadly,

Heu patior telis vulnera facta meis!

On the other side of the hedge sate one that heard his sorrow: who getting ouer, came towards him, and / brake off his passion. When he [D4 approached, hee saluted *Roberto* in this sort.

Gentleman quoth hee (for so you seeme) I haue by chaunce heard you discourse some part of your greefe; which appeareth to be more than you will discouer, or I can conceipt. But if you vouchsafe such simple comforte as my abilitie may yeeld, assure your selfe, that I wil indeuour to doe the best, that either may procure you profite, or bring you pleasure: the rather, for that I suppose you are a scholler, and pittie it is men of learning should liue in lacke.

Roberto wondring to heare such good wordes, for that this iron age affoordes few that esteeme of vertue; returnd him thankfull gratulations, and (vrgde by necessitie) vttered his present griefe, beseeching his aduise how he might be imployed. Why, easily quoth hee, and greatly to your benefite: for men of my profession gette by schollers their whole liuing. What is your profession, said *Roberto*? Truly sir, saide hee, I am a player. A player, quoth *Roberto*, I tooke you rather for a Gentleman of great liuing, for if by outward habit men should be censured, I tell you, you would bee taken for a substantiall man. So am I where I dwell (quoth the player) reputed able at my proper cost to build a Windmill. What though the world once went hard with me, when I was faine to carry my playing Fardle a footebacke; *Tempora mutantur*, I know you know the meaning of it better than I, but I thus conster it, its otherwise now; for my very share in playing apparell will not be sold for two hundred pounds.

Truly (said *Roberto*) tis straunge, that you should so prosper in that vayne practise, for that it seemes to mee your voice is nothing / gratious. Nay [D4ᵛ then, saide the Player, I mislike your iudgement: why, I am as famous for Delphrigus, & the King of Fairies, as euer was any of my time. The twelue labors of Hercules haue I terribly thundred on the Stage, and plaid three Scenes of the Deuill in the High way to heauen. Haue ye so (saide *Roberto*?) then I pray you pardon me. Nay more (quoth the Player) I can serue to make a pretie speech, for I was a countrey Author, passing at a Morrall, for twas I that pende the Morrall of mans witte, the Dialogue of Diues, and for seuen yeers space was absolute Interpreter to the puppets. But now my Almanacke is out of date:

> *The people make no estimation,*
> *Of Morrals teaching education.*

Was not this prettie for a plaine rime extempore? if ye will ye shall haue more. Nay its enough, said *Roberto*, but how meane you to vse mee? Why sir, in making Playes, said the other, for which you shall be well paid, if you will take the paines.

Roberto perceiuing no remedie, thought best in respect of his present necessitie, to try his wit, & went with him willingly: who lodgd him at the Townes end in a house of retayle, where what happened our Poet, you shall after heare. There

GROATSWORTH OF WITTE 35

by conuersing with bad company, he grew *A malo in peius*, falling from one vice to another: and so hauing founde a vaine to finger crowns, he grew cranker than *Lucanio*, who by this time began to droope, beeing thus dealt with by *Lamilia*. Shee hauing bewitched him with hir enticing wiles, caused him to consume in lesse than two yeeres that infinite treasure gathered by his father with so many a poore mãs curse. His lands sold, his iewels pawnd, his money wasted, he / was casseerd [E1 by *Lamilia*, that had coossend him of all. Then walkt he like one of Duke *Humfreys* Squires, in a thread-bare cloake, his hose drawne out with his heeles, his shooes vnseamed, least his feete should sweate with heat: now (as witlesse as hee was) he remembred his Fathers words, his vnkindnes to his brother, his carelesnes of himselfe. In this sorrow he sate down on pennilesse bench; where when *Opus* and *Vsus* told him by the chymes in his stomacke it was time to fall vnto meat, he was faine with the *Camelion* to feed vpon the aire, and make patience his best repast.

While he was at this feast, *Lamilia* came flaunting by, garnished with the iewels wherof she beguiled him, which sight serued to close his stomacke after his cold cheare. *Roberto* hearing of his brothers beggery, albeit he had little remorse of his miserable state, yet did seeke him out, to vse him as a propertie, whereby *Lucanio* was somewhat prouided for. But beeing of simple nature, hee serued but for a blocke to whet *Robertoes* wit on: which the poore foole perceiuing, he forsooke all other hopes of life, and fell to be a notorious Pandar, in which detested course he continued till death. But *Roberto* now famozed for an Arch-plaimaking-poet, his purse like the sea somtime sweld, anon like the same sea fell to a low ebbe; yet seldom he wanted, his labors were so well esteemed. Marry this rule he kept, what euer he fingerd afore hand, was the certaine meanes to vnbinde a bargaine, and being askt why hee so slightly dealt with them that did him good? It becoms me, saith hee, to bee contrary to the worlde; for commonly when vulgar men receiue earnest, they doo performe, when I am paid any thing afore-hand, I breake my promise. / He had [E1ᵛ shift of lodgings, where in euery place his Hostesse writ vp the wofull remembrance of him, his laundresse, and his boy; for they were euer his in housold, beside retainers in sundry other places. His companie were lightly the lewdest persons in the land, apt for pilferie, periurie, forgerie, or any villainy. Of these hee knew the casts to cog at cards, coossen at Dice; by these he learnd the legerdemaines of nips, foystes, connycatchers, crosbyters, lifts, high Lawyers, and all the rabble of that vncleane generation of vipers: and pithily could he paint out their whole courses of craft:

So cunning he was in all craftes, as nothing rested in him almost but craftines. How often the Gentlewoman his Wife labored vainely to recall him, is lamentable to note: but as one giuen ouer to all lewdnes, he communicated her sorrowfull lines among his loose truls, that iested at her bootlesse laments. If he could any way get credite on scores, he would then brag his creditors carried stones, comparing euery round circle to a groning O procured by a painfull burden. The shamefull ende of sundry his consorts deseruedly punished for their amisse, wrought no compunction in his heart: of which one, brother to a Brothell hee kept, was trust vnder a tree as round as a Ball.

To some of his swearing companions thus it happened: A crue of them sitting in a Tauerne carowsing, it fortuned an honest Gentleman and his friend, to enter their roome: some of them beeing acquainted with him, in their domineering drunken vaine would haue no nay but downe hee must needes sitte with them; beeing placed, no remedie there was, but he must needes keepe euen compasse with their vnseemely carrowsing. / [E2 Which he refusing, they fell from high words to sound strokes, so that with much adoo the Gentleman saued his owne, and shifted from their company. Being gone one of these tiplers forsooth lackt a gold Ring, the other sware they see the Gentleman take it from his hande. Vpon this the

Gentleman was indited before a Iudge, these honest men are deposde: whose wisedome weighing the time of the braule, gaue light to the Iury, what power wine-washing poyson had, they according vnto conscience found the Gentleman not guiltie, and God released by that verdit the innocent.

With his accusers thus it fared: One of them for murder was worthily executed: the other neuer since prospered: the third, sitting not long after vpon a lustie horse, the beast sodenly dyde vnder him, God amend the man.

Roberto euery day acquainted with these examples, was notwithstanding nothing bettered, but rather hardened in wickednesse. At last was that place iustified, God warneth men by dreams and visions in the night, and by knowne examples in the day, but if hee returne not, hee comes vppon him with iudgement that shall bee felt. For now when the number of deceites caused *Roberto* bee hatefull almost to all men, his immeasurable drinking had made him the perfect Image of the dropsie, and the loathsome scourge of Lust tyrannized in his bones: lying in extreame pouerty, and hauing nothing to pay but chalke, which now his Host accepted not for currant, this miserable man lay comfortlesly languishing, hauing but one groat left (the iust proportion of his Fathers Legacie) which looking on, he cryed: O now it is too late, too late to buy witte with thee: and therefore / will I see if I can sell to carelesse youth [E2ᵛ] what I negligently forgot to buy.

Heere (Gentlemen) breake I off *Robertoes* speach; whose life in most parts agreeing with mine, found one selfe punishment as I haue doone. Heereafter suppose me the saide *Roberto*, and I will goe on with that hee promised: *Greene* will send you now his groats-worth of wit, that neuer shewed a mites-worth in his life: & though no man now bee by to doo mee good: yet ere I die I will by my repentaunce indeuour to doo all men good.

Deceiuing world, that with alluring toyes,
Hast made my life the subiect of thy scorne :
And scornest now to lend thy fading ioyes,
To length my life, whom friends haue left forlorne.
How well are they that die ere they be borne,
   Ane neuer see thy sleights, which few men shun,
   Till vnawares they helpelesse are vndone.

Oft haue I sung of Loue, and of his fire,
But now I finde that Poet was aduizde ;
Which made full feasts increasers of desire,
And proues weake loue was with the poore despizde.
For when the life with food is not suffizde,
   What thought of Loue ; what motion of delight ;
   VVhat pleasance can proceed from such a wight?

VVitnesse my want, the murderer of my wit;
My rauisht sence of wonted furie reft;
VVants such conceit, as should in Poems fit
Set downe the sorrow wherein I am left: | [E3
But therefore haue high heauens their gifts bereft:
  Because so long they lent them mee to vse,
  And I so long their bountie did abuse.

O that a yeare were graunted me to liue,
And for that yeare my former wits restorde:
VVhat rules of life, what counsell would I giue?
How should my sinne with sorrow be deplorde?
But I must die of euery man abhorde.
  Time loosely spent will not againe be wonne,
  My time is loosely spent, and I vndone.

O *horrenda fames,* how terrible are thy assaults? but *vermis conscientiæ,* more woūding are thy stings. Ah Gentlemen, that liue to read my broken and confused lines, looke not I should (as I was wont) delight you with vaine fantasies, but gather my follies altogether; and as yee would deale with so many parricides, cast them into the fire: call them *Telegones,* for now they kil their Father, and euery lewd line in them written, is a deepe piercing wound to my heart; euery idle houre spent by any in reading them, brings a million of sorrowes to my soule. O that the teares of a miserable man (for neuer any man was yet more miserable) might wash their memorie out with my death; and that those works with mee together might bee interd. But sith they cannot, let this my last worke witnes against them with mee, how I detest them. Blacke is the remembrance of my blacke workes, blacker than night, blacker than death, blacker than hell.

Learne wit by my repentance (Gentlemen) and let these few rules following be regarded in your liues. /   [E3ᵛ

1 First in al your actions set God before your eies; for the feare of the Lord is the beginning of wisdome: Let his word be a lanterne to your feet, and a light vnto your paths, then shall you stand as firme rocks, and not be mocked.

2 Beware of looking backe, for God will not bee mocked; and of him that hath receiued much, much shal be demaunded.

3 If thou be single, and canst abstain, turne thy eies from vanitie; for there is a kinde of women bearing the faces of Angels, but the hearts of Deuils, able to intrap the elect if it were possible.

4 If thou bee married, forsake not the wife of thy youth to follow straunge flesh; for whoremongers and adulterers the Lord will iudge. The doore of a harlot leadeth downe to death, and in her lips there dwels destruction; her face is decked with odors, but she bringeth a man to a morsell of bread and nakednes: of which my selfe am instance.

D

5 If thou be left rich, remember those that want, & so deale, that by thy wilfulnes thy selfe want not: Let not Tauerners and Victuallers be thy Executors; for they will bring thee to a dishonorable graue.

6 Oppresse no man; for the crie of the wronged ascendeth to the eares of the Lord: neyther delight to increase by Vsurie, least thou loose thy habitation in the euerlasting Tabernacle.

7 Beware of building thy house to thy neighbors hurt; for the stones will crie to the timber; Wee were laid together in bloud: and those that so erect houses, calling them by their names, shall lie in the graue lyke Sheepe, and death shall gnaw vpon their soules. / [E4

8 If thou be poore, be also patient, and striue not to grow rich by indirect meanes; for goods so gotten shal vanish like smoke.

9 If thou bee a Father, Maister, or Teacher, ioyne good example with good counsaile; else little auaile precepts, where life is different.

10 If thou be a Sonne or Seruant, despise not reproofe; for though correction bee bitter at the first, it bringeth pleasure in the end.

Had I regarded the first of these rules, or beene obedient to the last; I had not now at my last ende, beene left thus desolate. But now, though to my selfe I giue *Consilium post facta*; yet to others they may serue for timely precepts. And therefore (while life giues leaue) I will send warning to my olde consorts, which haue liued as loosely as my selfe, albeit weaknesse will scarse suffer me to write, yet to my fellow Schollers about this Cittie, will I direct these few insuing lines.

To those Gentlemen his Quondam acquaintance, that spend their wits in making plaies, R. G. wisheth a better exercise, and wisdome to preuent his extremities.

IF wofull experience may moue you (Gentlemen) to beware, or vnheard of wretchednes intreate you to take heed: I doubt not but you wil looke backe with sorrow on your time past, and indeuour with repentance to spend that which is to come. Wonder not, (for with thee wil I first begin) thou famous gracer of Tragedians, that *Greene*, who hath said with thee (like the foole in his heart) There is no God, shoulde now giue / [E4ᵛ] glorie vnto his greatnes: for penetrating is his power, his hand lyes heauie vpon me, hee hath spoken vnto mee with a voice of thunder, and I haue felt he is a God that can punish enemies. Why should thy excellent wit, his gift, bee so blinded, that thou shouldst giue no glorie to the giuer? Is it pestilent Machiuilian pollicy that thou hast studied? O peeuish follie! What are his rules but

meere confused mockeries, able to extirpate in
small time the generation of mankind. For if *Sic
volo, sic iubeo*, hold in those that are able to com-
maund: and if it be lawfull *Fas & nefas* to do any
thing that is beneficiall; onely Tyrants should
possesse the earth, and they striuing to exceed in
tyrannie, should each to other be a slaughter man;
till the mightiest outliuing all, one stroke were
lefte for Death, that in one age mans life should
end. The brocher of this Diabolicall Atheisme is
dead, and in his life had neuer the felicitie hee
aymed at: but as he began in craft; liued in feare,
and ended in despaire. *Quàm inscrutabilia sunt Dei
iudicia?* This murderer of many brethren, had his
conscience seared like *Caine*: this betrayer of him
that gaue his life for him, inherited the portion of
Iudas: this Apostata perished as ill as *Iulian*: and
wilt thou my friend be his disciple? Looke but to
me, by him perswaded to that libertie, and thou
shalt find it an infernall bondage. I knowe the
least of my demerits merit this miserable death,
but wilfull striuing against knowne truth, ex-
ceedeth all the terrors of my soule. Defer not (with
me) till this last point of extremitie; for little
knowst thou how in the end thou shalt be visited.

With thee I ioyne yong *Iuuenall*, that byting
Satyrist, that lastly with mee together writ a
Comedie. / Sweet boy, might I aduise thee, be [F1
aduisde, and get not many enemies by bitter

wordes: inueigh against vaine men, for thou canst do it, no man better, no man so well: thou hast a libertie to reprooue all, and name none; for one being spoken to, all are offended; none being blamed no man is iniured. Stop shallow water still running, it will rage, or tread on a worme and it will turne: then blame not Schollers vexed with sharpe lines, if they reproue thy too much liberty of reproofe.

And thou no lesse deseruing than the other two, in some things rarer, in nothing inferiour; driuen (as my selfe) to extreme shifts, a litle haue I to say to thee: and were it not an idolatrous oth, I would sweare by sweet S. George, thou art vnworthy better hap, sith thou dependest on so meane a stay. Base minded men all three of you, if by my miserie you be not warnd: for vnto none of you (like mee) sought those burres to cleaue: those Puppets (I meane) that spake from our mouths, those Anticks garnisht in our colours. Is it not strange, that I, to whom they all haue beene beholding: is it not like that you, to whome they all haue beene beholding, shall (were yee in that case as I am now) bee both at once of them forsaken? Yes trust them not: for there is an vpstart Crow, beautified with our feathers, that with his *Tygers hart wrapt in a Players hyde*, supposes he is as well able to bombast out a blanke verse as the best of you: and beeing an absolute *Iohannes fac totum*, is in his owne conceit

the onely Shake-scene in a countrey. O that I
might intreat your rare wits to be imploied in more
profitable courses: & let those Apes imitate your
past excellence, and neuer more acquaint them
with your admired inuentions. I knowe the best
husband of/you all will neuer proue an Vsurer, [F1ᵛ
and the kindest of them all will neuer proue a kind
nurse: yet whilest you may, seeke you better
Maisters; for it is pittie men of such rare wits,
should be subiect to the pleasure of such rude
groomes.

In this I might insert two more, that both haue
writ against these buckram Gentlemen: but lette
their owne workes serue to witnesse against their
owne wickednesse, if they perseuere to maintaine
any more such peasants. For other new-commers,
I leaue them to the mercie of these painted monsters, who (I doubt not) will driue the best
minded to despise them: for the rest, it skils not
though they make a ieast at them.

But now returne I againe to you three, knowing
my miserie is to you no newes: and let mee hartily
intreat you to be warned by my harms. Delight
not (as I haue done) in irreligious oathes; for from
the blasphemers house, a curse shall not depart.
Despise drunkennes, which wasteth the wit, and
maketh men all equall vnto beasts. Flie lust, as the
deathsman of the soule, and defile not the Temple
of the holy Ghost. Abhorre those Epicures, whose

loose life hath made religion lothsome to your eares: and when they sooth you with tearms of Maistership, remember *Robert Greene*, whome they haue often so flattered, perishes now for want of comfort. Remember Gentlemen, your liues are like so many lighted Tapers, that are with care deliuered to all of you to maintaine: these with wind-puft wrath may be extinguisht, which drunkennes put out, which negligence let fall: for mans time is not of it selfe so short, but it is more shortned by sinne. The fire of my light is now at the last snuffe, and for want of wherewith to su/staine it, there is no substance lefte for life to [F2 feede on. Trust not then (I beseech ye) to such weake staies: for they are as changeable in minde, as in many attyres. Wel, my hand is tyrde, and I am forst to leaue where I would begin: for a whole booke cannot containe their wrongs, which I am forst to knit vp in some fewe lines of words.

Desirous that you should liue,
though himselfe be dying:
Robert Greene.

Now to all men I bid farewel in like sort, with this conceited Fable of that olde Comedian *Aesope*.

AN Ant and a Grashopper walking together on a Greene, the one carelesly skipping, the other carefully prying what winters prouision was scattered in the way: the Grashopper scorning (as wantons will) this needlesse thrift (as hee tearmed it) reprooued him thus :

The greedy miser thirsteth still for gaine,
His thrift is theft, his weale works others woe :
That foole is fond which will in caues remaine,
VVhen mongst faire sweets he may at pleasure goe.

To this the Ant perceiuing the Grashoppers meaning, quickly replyde :

The thriftie husband spares what vnthrift spends,
His thrift no theft, for dangers to prouide :
Trust to thy selfe, small hope in vvant yeeld friends,
A caue is better than the deserts wide. | [F2ᵛ]

In short time these two parted, the one to his pleasure, the other to his labour. Anon Haruest grew on, and reft from the Grashopper his woonted moysture. Then weakly skipt hee to the medowes brinks: where till fell winter he abode. But storms continually powring, hee went for succour to the Ant his olde acquaintance, to whom hee had scarce discouered his estate, but the waspish little worme made this reply.

Packe hence (quoth he) thou idle lazie worme,
My house doth harbor no vnthriftie mates :

Thou scorndst to toile, & now thou feelst the storme,
And starust for food while I am fed with cates.
   Vse no intreats, I will relentlesse rest,
   For toyling labour hates an idle guest.

The Grashopper foodlesse, helplesse and strengthles, got into the next brooke, and in the yeelding sand digde for himselfe a pit: by which hee likewise ingrau'de this Epitaph.

When Springs greene prime arrayd me with delight,
And euery power with youthfull vigor fild,
Gaue strength to worke what euer fancie wild:
I neuer feard the force of winters spight.

When first I saw the sunne the day begin,
And dry the Mornings tears from hearbs and grasse ;
I little thought his chearefull light would passe,
Till vgly night with darknes enterd in.
   And then day lost I mournd, spring past I wayld,
   But neither teares for this or that auailde. | [F3

Then too too late I praisd the Emmets paine,
That sought in spring a harbor gainst the heate :
And in the haruest gathered winters meat,
Preuenting famine, frosts, and stormy raine.

My wretched end may warn Greene springing youth
To vse delights, as toyes that will deceiue,

And scorne the world before the world them leaue :
For all worlds trust, is ruine without ruth.
    Then blest are they that like the toyling Ant,
    Prouide in time gainst winters wofull want.

With this the Grashopper yeelding to the wethers extremit, died comfortles without remedy. Like him my selfe: like me, shall all that trust to friends or times inconstancie. Now faint I of my last infirmity, beseeching them that shall burie my bodie, to publish this last farewell written with my wretched hand.

Fælicem fuisse infaustum.

A letter written to his wife, founde with this booke after his death.

The remembrance of the many wrongs offred thee, and thy vnreproued vertues, adde greater sorrow to my miserable state, than I can vtter or thou conceiue. Neither is it lessened by consideration of thy absence, (though shame would hardly let me behold thy face) but exceedingly aggrauated, for that I cannot (as I ought) to thy owne selfe reconcile my selfe, that thou mightst witnes my inward woe at this instant, that haue made / thee [F3ᵛ] a wofull wife for so long a time. But equall heauen hath denide that comfort, giuing at my last neede like succour as I haue sought all my life: being in this extremitie as voide of helpe, as thou hast beene of hope. Reason would, that after so long wast, I should not send thee a child to bring thee greater charge; but consider he is the fruit of thy wombe, in whose face regarde not the Fathers faults so much, as thy owne perfections. He is yet Greene, and may grow straight, if he be carefully tended: otherwise, apt enough (I feare mee) to follow his Fathers folly. That I haue offended thee highly I knowe, that thou canst forget my iniuries I hardly beleeue: yet perswade I my selfe, if thou saw my wretched estate, thou couldst not but lament it: nay certainly I know thou wouldst. All my wrongs muster themselues before mee, euery euill at once plagues mee. For my contempt of God, I am contemned of men: for my swearing and forswearing, no man will beleeue me: for my gluttony, I suffer hunger: for my drunkennes, thirst: for my adultery, vlcerous sores. Thus God hath cast me downe, that I might be humbled: and punished me for example of other sinners: and although he strangely suffers me in this world to perish without succor, yet trust I in the world to come to find mercie, by the merites of my Sauiour to whom I commend thee, and commit my soule.

Thy repentant husband for his disloyaltie, Robert Greene.

Fœlicem fuisse infaustum.

FINIS.

ERRATA

The following emendations only have been made in the text of the original:—

Page	Line		In the Original reads:
5	5	'pen:'	'pen?'
5	8	'worth:'	'worth?'
5	11	'selfe:'	'selfe?'
6	5	*'neuer'*	*'nener'*
9	17	'gold:'	'gold?'
9	19	'creature:'	'creature?'
10	8	'with)'	'with('
12	16	'wrong'	'worng'
12	25	'father),'	'father,'
27	2	'agreed: he'	'agreedh: e'
31	8	'anie'	'auie'
35	5	*'Lamilia'*	*'Laminia'*

The Repentance
of
ROBERT GREENE

Note

THE ORIGINAL of this text is in the Bodleian Library (Malone 575*). The few misprints which have been corrected in the text are noted on page 35.

G. B. H,

The Repentance
of Robert Greene Maister
of Artes.

Wherein by himselfe is laid open his loose life,
with the manner of his death.

AT LONDON,
Printed for Cutbert Burbie, and are to be sold at
the middle shop in the Poultry, vnder
Saint Mildreds Church.
1592.

The Printer to the Gentlemen Readers.

GENTLEMEN, I know you ar not vnacquainted with the death of *Robert Greene*, whose pen in his life time pleased you as well on the Stage, as in the Stationers shops: And to speake truth, although his loose life was odious to God and offensiue to men, yet forasmuch as at his last end he found it most grieuous to himselfe (as appeareth by this his repentant discourse) I doubt not but he shall for the same deserue fauour both of God and men. And considering Gentlemen that *Venus* hath her charmes to inchaunt; that Fancie is a Sorceresse bewitching the Senses, and follie the onely enemie to all vertuous actions. And forasmuch as the purest glasse is the most brickle, the finest Lawne the soonest staind, the highest Oake most subiect to the wind, and the quickest wit the more easily woone to folly: I doubt not but you will with regarde forget his follies, and like to the Bee gather hony out of the good counsels of him, who was wise, learned and polliticke, had not his lasciuious life withdrawen him from those studies which had been far more pro/fitable to [A2 him.

For herein appeareth that he was a man giuen ouer to the lust of his owne heart, forsaking all godlines & one that daily delighted in all manner of wickednes. Since other therefore haue forerun him in the like faults, and haue been forgiuen both of God and men I trust hee shall bee the better accepted, that by the working of Gods holy spirit, returnes with such a resolued Repentance, being a thing acceptable both to God and men.

To conclude, forasmuch as I found this discourse very passionate, and of woonderfull effect to withdraw the wicked from their vngodly waies, I thoght good to publish the same: and the rather, for that by his repentance they may as in a glasse see their owne follie, and thereby in time resolue, that it is better to die repentant, than to liue dishonest.

Yours C. B. / [A2ᵛ

To all the wanton youths of
England: *Robert Greene* wisheth refor-
mation of wilfulnes.

*W*HEN *I consider (kinde Cuntrimen) that youth is like to the spring time of mans age readie in the bloome to be nipped with euerie misfortune, and that a yong man is like to a tender plant, apt to be wrested by nurture either to good or euill, as his friendes like good Gardeners shall with care indeuour his education, seeing in the prime of our yeares vice is most ready to creepe in, and that want of experience committeth sundrie wanton desires, I thoght good to lay before you a president of such preiudiciall inconueniences, which at the first seeming sweete vnto youth, at the last growe into fruits of bitter repentance : For a yong man led on by selfe will (hauing the raines of libertie in his owne hand) foreseeth not the ruth of follie, but aimeth at present pleasures, for he giues himselfe vp to delight, and thinketh euerie thing good, honest, lawfull and vertuous, that fitteth for the content of his lasciuious humour: hee foreseeth not that such as clime hastely, fall sodainely : that Bees haue stings as well as honie : that vices haue ill endes as well as sweete beginnings : and whereof growes this heedles life, but of | selfe conceit, thinking the good* [A3 *counsell of age is dotage: that the aduice of friends proceeds of enuie, and not of loue : that when their* *fathers correct them for their faults, they hate them: whereas when the blacke Oxe hath trod on their feete, and the Crowes foote is seene in their eies, then toucht with the feeling of their owne follie, they sigh out had I wist, when repentance commeth too late. Or like as waxe is ready to receiue euerie newe fourme, that is stamped into it, so is youth apt to admit of euery vice that is obiected vnto it, and in young yeares wanton desires is cheefely predominate especiallie the two Ringleaders of all other mischiefes, namely pride and whoredome, these are the Syrens that with their inchanting melodies, drawe them on to vtter confusion, for after a young man hath suckt in that sinne of pride, hee groweth into contempt, and as he increaseth prowde in his attyre, so he is scornfull in his lookes, and disdaines the wholsome admonition of his honest freends, whose aduice he supposeth to be doone of malice, and therefore esteemeth his owne waies best, and had rather hazard his life, than to loose an intch of his credit. Pride is like to fier, that will die and goe out if it bee not maintained with fewell, and yet lay on neuer so bigge logges, it consumes them all to ashes, so pride craues maintenance, or els it will fade: and had a young man neuer so great reuenues, pride at last will reduce it to begger you, for it is such a sinne, as once got into the boane it will step into the flesh, he that once ietteth in his brauerie: if he haue no meanes to maintaine it, it will leaue no bad course of life vnattempted, but hee will haue corners to vphold his follie. Heereof growes coossenages, thefts, murthers, and a thousand*

other pettie mischiefes, and causes many pro | per [A3ᵛ
*persons to bee trust vp at the gallowes, purchasing
thereby infamy to themselues, and hart breaking
sorrow to their friends and parents for euer.*

*Companion to this vice, is lust and lecherie, which
is the viper, whose venome is incurable, and the onely
sinne that in this life leadeth vnto shame, and after
death vnto hell fire: for he that giueth himselfe ouer to
harlots, selleth his soule to destruction, and maketh his
bodie subiect to all incurable diseases. These two vices
do not onlie waste a mans substance, but also con-
sumeth his bodie and soule, and maketh him attempt to
do any mischiefe for his maintenance therein. If
happely the young man hath any grace, and is loth to
take any vnlawfull wayes, the ordinary course of his
copesmates, is straight to call him coward, and cast him
out of their fauour, or els by svveete persvvasions and
flattering vvordes, make him forsake God and all good
meanes of life vvhatsoeuer: this is the manner, life,
and course of such as vvill not listen to the graue
aduice of their parents, but seeke therby to bring their
graie haires vvith greefe vnto theyr graues.*

*This ensuing discourse, gentle Reader, dooth lay
open the graceles endeuours of my selfe, vvho although
I vvere for a long time giuen ouer to the lust of my ovvn
hart, yet in the end, Gods grace did so fauourablie
worke in me, that I trust heerein thou shalt perceiue
my true and vnfained repentance. Accept it in good
part, and if it may profit anie I haue my desire.*

                       Farewell, R. G. /   [A4

The Repentance
of Robert Greene, Maister
of Arts.

AS there is no steele so stiffe, but the stamp will pierce; no flint so harde, but the drops of raine will hollowe: so there is no heart so voide of grace, or giuen ouer to wilfull follie, but the mercifull fauour of God can mollifie. An instance of the like chaunced to my selfe, being a man wholy addicted to all gracelesse indeuors, giuen from my youth to wantonnes, brought vp in riot who as I grew in yeares, so I waxed more ripe in vngodlines, that I was the mirrour of mischiefe, and the very patterne of all preiudiciall actions: for I neither had care to take any good course of life, nor yet to listen to the friendly perswasions of my parents. I seemed as one of no religion, but rather as a meere Atheist, contemning the holy precepts vttered by any learned preacher: I would smile at such as would frequent the Church, or such place of godly exercise, & would scoffe at any that would checke mee with any wholesome or / good ad- [B1 monition: so that herein I seemed a meere reprobate, the child of Sathan, one wipt out of the booke of life, and as an outcast from the face and fauor of

God, I was giuen ouer to drunkennes, so that I lightly accounted of that company that would not intertaine my inordinate quaffing. And to this beastly sinne of gluttonie, I added that detestable vice of swearing, taking a felicitie in blaspeming & prophaning the name of God, confirming nothing idlely but with such solemne oths, that it amazed euen my companions to heare mee. And that I might seeme to heape one sinne vpon another, I was so rooted therein, that whatsoeuer I got, I stil consumed the same in drunkennes.

Liuing thus a long time, God (who suffereth sinners to heape coles of fire vpon their owne heads, and to bee fed fat with sinne against the day of vengeance) suffered me to go forward in my loose life: many warninges I had to draw me from my detestable kind of life, and diuers crosses to contrary my actions: but all in vaine, for though I were sundry times afflicted with many foule and greeuous diseases, and thereby scourged with the rod of Gods wrath, yet when by the great labor & frendship of sundry honest persons, they had (though to their great charges) sought & procured my recouery, I did with the Dog *Redire in vomitum*, I went again with the Sow to wallow in the mire, and fell to my former follies as frankly, as if I had not tasted any iot of want, or neuer been scourged for them. *Consuetudo peccandi tollit sensum peccati* ; my daily custome in sinne had cleane taken away the feeling of my sinne: for I was so giuen to these vices aforesaide, that I counted them rather veniall scapes & faults of nature, than any great / and greeuous offences: [Brᵛ neither did I care for death, but held it onely as the end of life. For comming one day into Aldersgate street to a welwillers house of mine, hee with other of his friendes perswaded me to leaue my bad course of life, which at length would bring mee to vtter destruction, whereupon I scoffingly made them this answer. Tush, what better is he that dies in his bed than he that endes his life at Tyburne, all owe God a death: if I may haue my desire while I liue, I am satisfied, let me shift after death as I may. My friends hearing these words, greatly greeued at my gracelesse resolution, made this reply: If you feare not death in this world, nor the paines of the body in this life, yet doubt the second death, & the losse of your soule, which without hearty repentance must rest in hell fire for euer and euer.

Hell (quoth I) what talke you of hell to me? I know if I once come there, I shal haue the company of better men than my selfe, I shal also meete with some madde knaues in that place, & so long as I shall not sit there alone, my care is the lesse. But you are mad folks (quoth I) for if I feared the Iudges of the bench no more than I dread the iudgements of God, I would before I slept diue into one Carles bagges or other, and make merrie with the shelles I found in them so long as they would last. And though some in this company were Fryers of mine owne fraternitie to whom I spake the wordes: yet were they so amazed at my prophane speeches, that they wisht themselues foorth of my company. Whereby appeareth, that my continuall delight was in sinne, and that I made my selfe drunke with the dregges of mischiefe. But beeing departed thence vnto my lodging, / and now grown to the full, I was [B2 checked by the mightie hand of God: for *Sicknes* (the messenger of death) attached me, and tolde me my time was but short, and that I had not long to liue: whereupon I was vexed in mind, and grew very heauy. As thus I sate solempnly thinking of my end, and feeling my selfe waxe sicker and sicker, I fell into a great passion, and was wonderfully perplexed, yet no way discouered my agony, but sate still calling to mind the lewdnes of my former life: at what time sodainly taking the booke of *Resolution* in my hand, I light vpon a chapter therein, which discouered vnto mee the miserable state of the reprobate, what Hell was, what the worme of Conscience was, what tormentes there was appointed for the damned soules, what vnspeakable miseries, what vnquenchable flames, what intollerable agonies, what incomprehensible griefs; that there was nothing but feare, horrour, vexation of mind, depriuation from the sight and fauour of God, weeping and gnashing of teeth, and that al those tortures were not termined or dated within any compasse of yeares, but euerlasting world without end; concluding all in this of the Psalmes: *Ab inferis nulla est redemptio.*

After that I had with deepe consideration pondered vpon these points, such a terrour stroke into my conscience, that for very anguish of minde my teeth did beate in my head, my lookes waxed pale and wan, and fetching a great sigh, I cried vnto God, and said: If all this be true, oh what shall become of me? If the rewarde of sinne be death and hell, how many deaths and hels do I deserue, that haue beene a most miserable sinner? If damnation be the meed for wickednes, then am I dam / ned? for in all the world there neuer liued [B2v a man of worser life. Oh what shall I doe? I cannot call to God for mercie; for my faultes are beyond the compasse of his fauour: the punishment of the body hath an ende by death, but the paines of the soule by death are made euerlasting. Then what a miserable case am I in if I die? yet if my death might redeeme my offences, & wash away my sinnes, oh might I suffer euery day twentie deathes while seuen yeares lasteth, it were nothing: but when I shall end a contempt to the world, I shal enioy the disdaine of men, the displeasure of God, & my soule (that immortall creature) shall euerlastingly bee damned: Oh woe is mee, why doe I liue? nay rather why was I borne? Cursed be the day wherein I was born, and haplesse be the brests that gaue me sucke. Why did God create me to bee a vessell of wrath? Why did hee breath life into me, thus to make me a lost sheepe? Oh I feele a hell already in my conscience, the number of my sinnes do muster before my eies, the poore mens plaints that I haue wronged, cries out in mine eares and saith, *Robin Greene* thou art damnd; nay, the iustice of God tels mee I cannot bee saued. Now I do remember (though too late) that I haue read in the Scriptures, how neither adulterers, swearers, theeues, nor murderers shall inherite the kingdome of heauen. What hope then can I haue of any grace, when (giuen ouer from all grace) I exceeded all other in these kinde of sinnes? If thus vppon earth and aliue I feele a hell, oh what a thing is that hell, where my soule shall euerlastingly liue in torments. I am taught by the scripture to pray; but to whom shoulde I pray? to him that I haue blasphemed, to him that I haue contemned and despised, / [B3 whose name I haue taken in vaine? No, no, I am in a hell. Oh that my last gaspe were come, that I might be with Iudas or Cain, for their place is better than mine; or that I might haue power with these hands to vnlose my soule from this wretched carcasse, that hath imprisoned so many wicked villainies within it. Oh I haue sinned, not against the Father, nor against the Sonne, but against the holy Ghost: for I presumed vpon grace, and when the spirit of God cried in my mind & thoght, and said, drunkennes is a vice, whoredome is a vice; I carelesly (in contempt) resisted this motion, and as it were in a brauery, committed these sinnes with greedines. Oh now I shall crie with Diues to haue one drop of water for my tongue, but shall not be heard: I haue sinned against my owne soule, and therefore shalbe cast into vtter darknesse: and further I shall not come till I haue paid the vttermost farthing, which I shal neuer be able to satisfie. O happy are you that feele the sparks of Gods fauour in your hearts, happy are you that haue hope in the passion of Christ, happy are you that beleue that God died for you, happy are you that can pray. Oh why doth not God shew the like mercie vnto mee? The reason is, because in all my life I neuer did any good. I alwaies gloried in sinne, and despised them that imbraced vertue. God is iust, and cannot pardon my offences; and therefore I would I were out of this earthly hell, so I were in that second hell, that my soule might suffer tormentes: for now I am vexed both in soule and bodie.

In this despairing humor, searching further into the said Booke of *Resolution*, I found a place that greatly did comfort mee, & laid before me the promises of Gods / mercie, shewing mee that [B3ᵛ] although the Iustice of God was great to punish sinners, yet his mercie did exceede his works: and though my faults were as red as skarlet, yet washt with his bloud, they shoulde bee made as white as snow: therein was laid before mine eyes, that Dauid (who was called a man after his owne heart) did both commit adultery, and sealde it with murther: yet when hee did repent, God heard him, and admited him to his fauour. Therin was laid before me the obstinate sinne of Peter, that not onely denied his Maister Christ, but also forswore himselfe: yet so soone as hee shed tears, and did hartily repent him, his offences were pardoned. Therein was laid open the theefe that had liued licentiously, and had scarse in all his life done one good deed, and yet hee was saued by hope in the mercies of God. Therein was also laide open how the seueritie of the Law was mittigated with the sweet and comfortable promises of the Gospell, insomuch that I began to be somewhat pacified, & a little quieted in mind, taking great ioy and comfort in the pithie perswasions and promises of Gods mercie alleadged in that Booke. And yet I was not presently resolued in my conscience, that God would deale so fauorably with me, for that stil the multitude of my sinnes presented me with his Iustice: and would therefore reason thus with my selfe. Why, those men (before mentioned) were elected and predestinated to be chosen vessels of Gods glory, & therfore though they did fal, yet they rose againe, & did shew it in time, with some other fruits of their election. But contrariwise, I (the most wicked of all men) was euen brought vp from my swadling clouts in wickednes, my infancy was sin, & my riper age increast in wickednes; I/[B4 tooke no pleasure but in ill, neither was my minde sette vpon any thing but vpon the spoyle: then seeing all my life was lead in lewdnes, and I neuer but once felt any remorse of conscience, how can God pardon mee, that repent rather for feare then for loue? Yet calling vnto mind the words of *Esay*, that at what time soeuer a sinner doth repent him from the bottome of his heart, the Lord would wipe away all his wickednes out of his remembrance.

Thus beeing at a battaile betweene the spirite and the flesh, I beganne to feele a greater comfort in my mind, so that I did [with] teares confesse and acknowledge, that although I was a most miserable sinner, yet the anguish that Christ suffered on the Crosse, was able to purge and cleanse me from all my offences: so that taking hold with faith vpon the promises of the Gospell, I waxed strong in spirite, and became able to resist and withstand all the desperate attempts that Sathan had giuen before to my weake and feeble conscience. When

thus I had consideratly thought on the wretchednes of my life, and therewithall looked into the
vncertainty of death, I thought good to
write a short discourse of the same,
which I haue ioyned to this
treatise, containing as
followeth. / [B4ᵛ

The life and death
of Robert Greene Maister
of Artes.

I NEEDE not make long discourse of my parentes, who for their grauitie and honest life is well knowne and esteemed amongst their neighbors; namely, in the Cittie of Norwitch, where I was bred and borne. But as out of one selfe same clod of clay there sprouts both stinking weeds and delightfull flowers: so from honest parentes often grow most dishonest children; for my Father had care to haue mee in my Non-age brought vp at schoole, that I might through the studie of good letters grow to be a frend to my self, a profitable member to the common-welth, and a comfort to him in his age. But as early pricks the tree that will proue a thorne: so euen in my first yeares I began to followe the filthines of mine owne desires, and neyther to listen to the wholesome aduertisements of my parentes, nor bee rulde by the carefull correction of my Maister. For being at the Vniuersitie of Cambridge, I / light amongst wags [C1 as lewd as my selfe, with whome I consumed the flower of my youth, who drew mee to trauell into

Italy, and Spaine, in which places I sawe and practizde such villainie as is abhominable to declare. Thus by their counsaile I sought to furnish my selfe with coine, which I procured by cunning sleights from my Father and my friends, and my Mother pampered me so long, and secretly helped mee to the oyle of Angels, that I grew thereby prone to all mischiefe: so that beeing then conuersant with notable Braggarts, boon companions and ordinary spend-thrifts, that practized sundry superficiall studies, I became as a Sien grafted into the same stocke, whereby I did absolutely participate of their nature and qualities. At my return into England, I ruffeled out in my silks, in the habit of *Malcontent*, and seemed so discontent, that no place would please me to abide in, nor no vocation cause mee to stay my selfe in: but after I had by degrees proceeded Maister of Arts, I left the Vniuersitie and away to London, where (after I had continued some short time, & driuen my self out of credit with sundry of my frends) I became an Author of Playes, and a penner of Loue Pamphlets, so that I soone grew famous in that qualitie, that who for that trade growne so ordinary about London as *Robin Greene*. Yong yet in yeares, though olde in wickednes, I began to resolue that there was nothing bad, that was profitable: whereupon I grew so rooted in all mischiefe, that I had as great a delight in wickednesse, as sundrie hath in godlinesse: and as much felicitie, I tooke in villainy, as others had in honestie.

Thus was the libertie I got in my youth, the cause / of my licentious liuing in my age, and [C1ᵛ beeing the first steppe to hell, I find it now the first let from heauen.

But I would wish all my natiue Countrymen, that reade this my repentaunce; First to feare God in their whole life, which I neuer did: Secondly, to obey their Parents, and to listen vnto the wholesome counsaile of their Elders: so shall their dayes be multiplied vppon them heere on earth, and inherite the crowne of glorie in the kingdome of heauen. I exhort them also to leaue the company of lewd and ill liuers: for conuersing with such Copes-mates, drawes them into sundry dangerous inconueniences: nor lette them haunt the company of harlots, whose throates are as smooth as oyle, but their feet lead the steps vnto death and destruction: for they like Syrens with their sweete inchaunting notes, soothed me vp in all kind of vngodlines.

Oh take heede of Harlots (I wish you the vnbridled youth of England) for they are the Basiliskes that kill with their eyes, they are the Syrens that allure with their sweete lookes; and they leade their fauorers vnto their destruction, as a sheepe is lead vnto the slaughter.

From whordome I grew to drunkennes, from

drunkennes to swearing and blaspheming the name of God, hereof grew quarrels, frayes, and continual controuersies, which are now as wormes in my conscience gnawing incessantly. And did I not through hearty repentance take hold of Gods mercies, euen these detestable sinnes woulde drench me downe into the damnable pit of destruction; for *Stipendium peccati mors.*

Oh knowe (good Countrymen) that the horrible sins and intollerable blasphemie I haue vsed against the / Maiestie of God, is a blocke in my [C2 conscience, and that so heauy that there were no way with me but desperation, if the hope of Christs death and passion did not helpe to ease mee of so intollerable and heauie a burthen.

I haue long with the deafe Adder stopt mine eares against the voice of Gods Ministers, yea my heart was hardened with Pharao against all the motions that the spirit of God did at any time worke in my mind, to turn me from my detestable kind of liuing.

Yet let me confesse a trueth, that euen once, and yet but once, I felt a feare and horrour in my conscience, & then the terrour of Gods iudgementes did manifestly teach me that my life was bad, that by sinne I deserued damnation, and that such was the greatnes of my sinne, that I deserued no redemption. And this inward motion I receiued in Saint Andrews Church in the Cittie of Norwich, at a Lecture or Sermon then preached by a godly learned man, whose doctrine, and the maner of whose teaching, I liked wonderfull well: yea (in my conscience) such was his singlenes of hart, and zeale in his doctrine, that hee might haue conuerted the most monster of the world.

Well, at that time, whosoeuer was worst, I knewe my selfe as bad as he: for being new come from Italy, (where I learned all the villanies vnder the heauens) I was drownd in pride, whoredome was my daily exercise, and gluttony with drunkennes was my onely delight.

At this Sermon the terrour of Gods iudgementes did manifestly teach me, that my exercises were damnable, and that I should bee wipte out of the booke of life, if I did not speedily repent my loosenes of life, and re / forme my mis- [C2v] demeanors.

At this Sermon the said learned man (who doubtles was the child of God) did beate downe sinne in such pithie and perswasiue manner, that I began to call vnto mind the daunger of my soule, and the preiudice that at length would befall mee for those grosse sinnes which with greedines I daily committed: in so much as sighing I said in my selfe, Lord haue mercie vpon mee, and send me grace to amend and become a new man.

But this good motion lasted not long in mee; for no sooner had I met with my copesmates, but seeing me in such a solemne humour, they demaunded the cause of my sadnes: to whom when I had discouered that I sorrowed for my wickednesse of life, and that the Preachers wordes had taken a deepe impression in my conscience, they fell vpon me in ieasting manner, calling me Puritane and Presizian, and wished I might haue a Pulpit, with such other scoffing tearmes, that by their foolish perswasion the good and wholesome lesson I had learned went quite out of my remembrance: so that I fel againe with the Dog to my olde vomit, and put my wicked life in practise, and that so throughly as euer I did before.

Thus although God sent his holy spirit to call mee, and though I heard him, yet I regarded it no longer than the present time, when sodainly forsaking it, I went forward obstinately in my misse. Neuerthelesse soone after I married a Gentlemans daughter of good account, with whom I liued for a while: but forasmuch as she would perswade me from my wilfull wickednes, after I had a child by her, I cast her off, hauing spent vp the marriage money which I obtained by her. / [C3]

Then left I her at six or seuen, who went into Lincolneshire, and I to London: where in short space I fell into fauor with such as were of honorable and good calling. But heere note, that though I knew how to get a friend, yet I had not the gift or reason how to keepe a friend: for hee that was my dearest friend, I would bee sure so to behaue my selfe towards him, that he shoulde euer after professe to bee my vtter enemie, or else vowe neuer after to come in my company.

Thus my misdemeanors (too many to bee recited) caused the most part of those so much to despise me, that in the end I became friendles, except it were in a fewe Alehouses, who commonly for my inordinate expences would make much of me, vntil I were on the score, far more than euer I meant to pay by twenty nobles thick. After I had wholy betaken me to the penning of plaies (which was my continuall exercise) I was so far from calling vpon God, that I sildome thought on God, but tooke such delight in swearing and blaspheming the name of God, that none could thinke otherwise of mee, than that I was the child of perdition.

These vanities and other trifling Pamphlets I penned of Loue, and vaine fantasies was my chiefest stay of liuing, and for those my vaine discourses, I was beloued of the more vainer sort of people, who beeing my continuall companions, came still to my lodging, and there would continue quaffing, carowsing, and surfeting with me all the day long.

But I thanke God, that hee put it in my head, to lay open the most horrible coosenages of the common Conny-catchers, Cooseners, and Crossebiters, which I haue indifferently handled in those my seuerall discour / ses already imprinted. [C3ᵛ And my trust is, that those discourses will doe great good, and bee very beneficiall to the Commonwealth of England.

But oh my deare Wife, whose company and sight I haue refrained these sixe years: I aske God and thee forgiuenesse for so greatly wronging thee, of whome I seldome or neuer thought, vntill now: Pardon mee (I pray thee) where soeuer thou art, and God forgiue mee all my offences.

And now to you all that liue and reuell in such wickednesse as I haue done, to you I write, and in Gods name wish you to looke to your selues, and to reforme your selues for the safegard of your owne soules: dissemble not with God, but seeke grace at his handes, hee hath promist it, and he will performe it.

God doth sundry times deferre his punishment vnto those that runne a wicked race; but *Quod defertur non aufertur*, that which is deferde is not quittanst, a day of reckoning will come, when the Lord will say; *Come giue account of thy Stewardship*. What God determineth, man cannot preuent: he that binds two sinnes together, cannot go vnpunisht in the one: so long the Pot goeth to the Pit, that at last it comes broken home.

Therefore (all my good friends) hope not in money, nor in friends, in fauors, in kindred, they are all vncertaine, and they are furthest off, when men thinke them most nigh. Oh were I now to begin the flower of my youth, were I now in the prime of my yeares, how far would I bee from my former follyes? what a reformed course of life would I take: but it is too late; onely now the comfortable mercies of the Lord is left me to hope in. / [C4

It is bootlesse for me to make any long discourse to such as are gracelesse as I haue beene, all wholesome warninges are odious vnto them, for they with the spider sucke poison out of the most pretious flowers, & to such as God hath in his secrete councell elected, fewe words will suffize. But howsoeuer my life hath beene, let my repentant ende be a generall example to all the youth in England to obey their parentes, to flie whoredome, drunkennes, swearing, blaspheming, contempt of the word, and such greeuous and grosse sinnes, least they bring their parents heads with sorrow to their graues, and least (with mee) they be a blemish to their kindred, and to their posteritie for euer.

Thus may you see how God hath secrete to himselfe the times of calling, and when hee will haue them into his vineyard, some hee calles in the morning, some at noone, and some in the euening, and yet hath the last his wages as well as the first: For as his iudgementes are inscrutable, so are his mercies incomprehensible. And therefore let all men learne these two lessons; not to despaire, because God may worke in them through his spirit at the last houre; nor to presume, least God giue them ouer for their presumption, and deny them repentance, and so they die impenitent: which *finalis impenitentia* is a manifest sinne against the holy Ghost.

To this doth that golden sentence of S. *Augustine* allude, which hee speaketh of the theefe hanging on the Crosse. *There was* (saith hee) *one theefe saued and no more, therefore presume not ; and there was one saued, and therefore despaire not*. And to conclude, take these caueats hereafter following. /
[C4ᵛ

Certaine Cauiats sent by Ro-
bert Greene to a frend of his (as a farewell:)
written with his owne hande.

1 THE feare of the Lord is the beginning of wisdome: therfore serue God, least he suffer thee to be lead into temptation.

2 Despise neither his worde nor his Minister: for he that heareth not can haue no faith, & without faith no man can be saued.

3 Obey thy Prince: for he that lifteth his hande against the Lords anointed, shall be like vnto a withered plant.

4 Despise not the counsaile of thy Father, nor the wholesome admonition of thy mother: for he that listeneth not to their lessons, shall be cut off in his youth.

5 Spend the prime of thy yeares in vertue: so dost thou lay an earnest pennie of honorable age.

6 Flie the sweetnes of the grape: for a man that is giuen to much wine shall neuer be rich.

7 Take not the name of God in vaine: for then thou shalt not bee guiltlesse, nor shall the curse of God come neare thy house.

8 A man that delights in harlots shall heape sinne vpon his soule: he shall be an open shame in the streets, and his place shall not be knowne. / [D1

9 He that robbeth from his neighbour, purchaseth discredit to himselfe and his kindred, and he shall not go to his graue with honor.

10 Who medleth with pitch shall be defiled, and he that eateth the bread of Robbers, fatneth himselfe against the day of vengeance.

11 Giue not thy youth ouer to the Deuill, neyther vow the dregs of thy olde age vnto God; for a repentant mind commeth from God.

12 Remember thy end, and thou shalt neuer doe amisse, and let the law of the Lord be a lanthorne to thy feete: so shall thy pathes bee aright, and thou die with honour.

Robert Greene. / [D1ᵛ

The manner of the death and last end of
Robert Greene Maister of Artes.

AFTER that he had pend the former discourse (then lying sore sicke of a surfet which hee had taken with drinking) hee continued most patient and penitent; yea, he did with teares forsake the world, renounced swearing, and desired forgiuenes of God and the worlde for all his offences: so that during all the time of his sicknesse (which was about a moneths space) hee was neuer heard to sweare, raue, or blaspheme the name of God as he was accustomed to do before that time, which greatly comforted his welwillers, to see how mightily the grace of God did worke in him.

He confessed himselfe that he was neuer heart sicke, but said that al his paine was in his belly. And although he continually scowred, yet still his belly sweld, and neuer left swelling vpward, vntill it sweld him at the hart and in his face.

During the whole time of his sicknes, he continually called vpon God, and recited these sentences following:

O Lord forgiue me my manifold offences.
O Lord haue mercie vpon me.
O Lord forgiue me my secret sinnes, and in thy mercie (Lord) pardon them all. /   [D2
Thy mercie (O Lord) is aboue thy works.

And with such like godly sentences hee passed the time, euen till he gaue vp the Ghost.

And this is to bee noted, that his sicknesse did not so greatly weaken him, but that he walked to his chaire & backe againe the night before he departed, and then (being feeble) laying him downe on his bed, about nine of the clocke at night, a friend of his tolde him, that his Wife had sent him commendations, and that shee was in good health: whereat hee greatly reioiced, confessed that he had mightily wronged her, and wished that hee might see her before he departed. Whereupon (feeling his time was but short), hee tooke pen and inke, & wrote her a Letter to this effect.

SWEET Wife, as euer there was any good will or friendship betweene thee and mee, see this bearer (my Host) satisfied of his debt, I owe him tenne pound, and but for him I had perished in the streetes. Forget and forgiue my wronges done vnto thee, and Almighty God haue mercie on my soule. Farewell till we meet in heauen, for on earth thou shalt neuer see me more.
This 2. of September.
1592.

VVritten by thy dying Husband

Robert Greene. / [D2ᵛ

Greenes Prayer in the time of
his sicknesse.

O LORD Iesus Christ my Sauiour and redeemer, I humbly beseech thee to looke downe from heauen vpon mee (thy seruant) that am grieued with thy spirite that I may patiently endure to the end thy rod of chastisement: And forasmuch as thou art Lorde of life and death, as also of strength, health, age, weakenes, and sicknes, I do therefore wholy submit my selfe vnto thee, to bee dealt withall according to thy holy will and pleasure. And seeing O mercifull Iesu, that my sinnes are innumerable like vnto the sandes of the sea, and that I haue so often offended thee that I haue worthely deserued death and vtter damnation, I humbly pray thee to deale with me according to thy gratious mercie and not agreeable to my wicked deserts. And graunt that I may (O Lorde) through thy spirite with patience, suffer and beare this Crosse, which thou hast worthily laid vppon mee: notwithstanding how greeuous soeuer the burthen thereof be, that my faith may be found laudable and glorious in thy sight, to the increase of thy glory, & my euerlasting felicitie. For euen thou (O Lord) most sweete Sauior didst first suffer paine before thou wert crucified: Since

therefore O meeke Lambe of God that my way to e/ternall ioy is to suffer with thee worldly gree- [D3 uances, graunt that I may be made like vnto thee, by suffering paciently, aduersitie, trouble, and sicknes. And lastly, forasmuch as the multitude of thy mercies doth put away the sinnes of those which truely repent, so as thou remembrest them no more, open the eye of thy mercie, and behold me a most miserable and wretched sinner, who for the same doth most earnestly desire pardon and forgiuenes. Renew (O Lorde) in mee, whatsoeuer hath beene decayed by the fraudulent mallice of Sathan, or my owne carnall wilfulnes: receiue me (O Lord) into thy fauour, consider of my contrition, and gather vp my teares into thy heauenly habitation: and seeing (O Lorde) my whole trust and confidence is onely in thy mercie, blot out my offences, and tread them vnder feet, so as they may not be a witnesse against me at the day of wrath. Grant this O Lord, I humbly beseech thee, for thy mercies sake.
Amen.

FINIS.